M000048256

Unit

From Here to There

Mc
Graw
Hill
Education

Contents

Get It Quick!

Ken Cavanagh/McGraw-Hill Education

Jim set a jug in a box.
Jim can jot on a tag.
Jim had to jam it in.

C Squared Studios/Getty Images, (vase) Diana Taliun/iStock/Getty Images

Paul Burns/Photodisc/Getty Images

Can it get to Jack quick?
Jan can do the job.

The box sat in the back.
Nick did not quit.

4

Martin Barraud/Getty Images

The box was on the jet.
Rex did not quit.

KatarzynaBialasiewicz/iStock/Getty Images

Jack can get the box.
"It is for me," said Jack.
"It got here quick."

Jen Is Quick!

Jen can hug the big jug.
Jen can jog to Kim.
"I am quick," said Jen.

Jen can get jam to Nan.
"Quack," said the fat duck.
"I am quick," said Jen.

"I am here," said Jen.
Mom can get to a job.
Jen can get on the bus.

Jen can sit in a big jet.
It can get up quick.
Jen can see the red sun.

Jen can not get on.
It is quick, quick, quick!

Yes, Zack Can Go!

Can Zack get in it?
Yes, Zack can.
Zack is on the bus.

The van bus is in mud.
Yuck! It can not go.
What can Zack do?

Yuck! Dot can get Max.
Max can fix it.
Can the bus go yet?

Can Zack get on this bus?
Yes, Zack can get on it.
It can go quick.

Zack can zip.
Zack can zig-zag.
Zack can run for fun!

Rex, Kim, and Zig

Yuck! This mud is red.
What can we do?
Can Rex do the job?

Yes, let Rex wet it.
Let Rex rub it.
Rex can fix it for us.

Can Kim do this job?
Yes, let us get in the cab.
Kim can get it to zip.

Kim can zip in the cab.
Kim can get us here.

Can Zig do this job?
Yes, Zig can mix it.
Yum, yum!

Zig-Zag Jet Can Zip

Here is the zig-zag jet.
It is red, big and quick.
Vick, Jan and Gus want fun.

Gus said, "Jan can fix it.
Jan can go with me.
Jan can not quit yet."

Gus got a tin can for gas.
What job can Jan fix?
Yes, Jan got gas in the jet.

It can zip, dip, and hum.
It can zig-zag up.
It can not quit!

This jet can win.
Vick, Gus and Jan can sit.
They have a lot of fun.

Get It Quick!

DECODABLE WORDS
Target Phonics Elements
Initial Consonant *j*, Initial Consonant *qu*; *j*: Jack, jam, jet, Jim, job, jot, jug; ***qu*:** quick, quit

HIGH-FREQUENCY WORDS
here, me
Review: a, do, for, is, said, the, to, was

Jen Is Quick!

DECODABLE WORDS
Target Phonics Elements
Initial Consonant *j*, Initial Consonant *qu*; *j*: jam, Jen, jet, job, jog, jug; ***qu*:** quack, quick, quit

HIGH-FREQUENCY WORDS
here
Review: a, I, is, said, see, the, to

Yes, Zack Can Go!

DECODABLE WORDS
Target Phonics Elements
Initial Consonant *y*, Initial Consonant *z*; *y*: yes, yuck, yet; ***z*:** Zack, zig-zag, zip

HIGH-FREQUENCY WORDS
this, what
Review: do, go, is, the

Rex, Kim, and Zig

DECODABLE WORDS
Target Phonics Elements
Initial Consonant *y*, Initial Consonant *z*; *y*: yes, yuck, yum; ***z*:** zig, zip

HIGH-FREQUENCY WORDS
this, what
Review: and, do, for, here, is, the, to, we

Zig-Zag Jet Can Zip!

DECODABLE WORDS
Target Phonics Elements
Review Letters *u*, *g*, *w*, *x*, *v*, *j*, *qu*, *z*, *y*: up, fun, Gus, hum; ***g*:** gas, get, Gus, big; ***w*:** win; ***x*:** fix; ***v*:** Vick; ***j*:** Jan, jet; ***qu*:** quick, quit; ***z*:** zig-zag, zip; ***y*:** yes, yet

HIGH-FREQUENCY WORDS
have, here, me, of, said, they, this, want, what
Review: and, go, is, the, with

HIGH-FREQUENCY WORDS TAUGHT TO DATE

Grade K

a
and
are
can
do
for
go
have
he
here
I
is
like
little
me
my
of
said
see
she
the
they
this
to
want
was
we
what
with
you

DECODING SKILLS TAUGHT TO DATE

Initial and final consonant *m*; short *a*; initial *s*; initial and final consonant *p*; initial and final consonant *t*; initial and medial vowel *i*; initial and final consonant *n*; initial *c*; initial and medial vowel *o*; initial and final *d*; initial consonant *h*; initial and medial vowel *e*; initial consonants *f* and *r*; initial and final consonant *b*; initial consonant *l*; initial consonant *k*; final digraph *ck*; initial and medial vowel *u*; initial and final *g*; initial *w*; final consonant *x*; initial consonant *v*; initial consonant *j*; initial consonant *qu*; initial consonant *z*; initial consonant *y*